JUNETEENTH

by Robin Nelson

first step nonfiction

Lerner Publications Company · Minneapolis

We **celebrate** Juneteenth
every year.

2009 — June

SUNDAY	MONDAY	TUESDAY	WEDNESDAY	THURSDAY	FRIDAY	SATURDAY
	1	2	3	4	5	6
7	8	9	10	11	12	13
14	15	16	17	18	19 Juneteenth	20
21	22	23	24	25	26	27
28	29	30				

This holiday is on June 19.

Juneteenth began many
years ago.

America was fighting about
slaves.

Many slaves were black
people who were owned by
white people.

Slaves had to **obey** their owner.

President Lincoln said that
slaves should be free.

But some slaves did not
know they had been freed.

It took two years for the last
slaves to hear the news.

These last slaves lived in Texas.

When they heard they were
free, they celebrated.

They sang and danced.

We still celebrate **freedom**
on Juneteenth.

We gather for picnics.

We watch parades.

We celebrate with friends,
family, and **neighbors**.

Juneteenth Timeline

1619
Black slaves
were first brought
to America.

June 19, 1865
Slaves in Texas
heard the news that
they were free.

January 1, 1863
President
Abraham Lincoln
freed slaves in
the rebel states.

June 19, 1866
The first Juneteenth celebration was held.

December 6, 1865
Slavery ends. Freedom for all slaves became a law.

January 1, 1980
Juneteenth became a state holiday in Texas.

Juneteenth Facts

 The last slaves to hear the news that they were free lived in Galveston, Texas.

 Juneteenth was also called Freedom Day, Emancipation Day, or Jubilee. It got the name Juneteenth from blending June and 19th.

 Juneteenth began in Texas. Then people who moved to other parts of the country brought the holiday with them. Now it is celebrated all over the country.

Red velvet cake and red soda pop are special Juneteenth treats.

The Civil War was the war that America fought over the slaves. Part of America thought slaves should be free and part did not. The Civil War began in 1861 and ended in 1865.

The order President Lincoln made to free slaves was called the Emancipation Proclamation. It became law on January 1, 1863.

Glossary

 celebrate – to have a party or special activity to honor a special occasion

 freedom – not being owned or controlled by others

 neighbors – people who live near you

 obey – to do what you are told

 slaves – people who are owned by another person

Index

The images in this book are used with the permission of: © Ralph Barrera/Austin American-Statesman/WpN/Photoshot, pp. 2, 16, 17, 22 (top and center); © Independent Picture Service, p. 3; © North Wind Picture Archives, p. 4; © Stock Montage/Hulton Archive/Getty Images, p. 5; © Private Collection/Peter Newark American Pictures/The Bridgeman Art Library International, pp. 6, 7, 22 (second from bottom); The Granger Collection, New York, pp. 8, 12; © Hulton Archive/Getty Images, pp. 9, 22 (bottom); © George Eastman House/Hulton Archive/Getty Images, p. 10; © Dorling Kindersley/Getty Images, p. 11; © Mansell/Time & Life Pictures/Getty Images, p. 13; © Bob Daemmrich/The Image Works, pp. 14, 22 (second from top); © Paul Barton/CORBIS, p. 15.
Front Cover: © Larry Kolvoor/Austin American-Statesman/WpN/Photoshot.

Lerner Publications Company
A division of Lerner Publishing Group, Inc.
241 First Avenue North
Minneapolis, MN 55401 U.S.A.

Website address: www.lernerbooks.com

Library of Congress Cataloging-in-Publication Data

Nelson, Robin, 1971–
    Juneteenth / by Robin Nelson.
        p.   cm. — (First step nonfiction. American holidays)
    Includes index.
    ISBN 978–0–7613–4934–1 (lib. bdg. : alk. paper)
    1. Juneteenth—Juvenile literature. 2. African Americans—Texas—Galveston—Social life and customs—Juvenile literature. 3. Slaves—Emancipation—United States—Juvenile literature. 4. African Americans—Anniversaries, etc.—Juvenile literature. 5. African Americans—Social life and customs—Juvenile literature. 6. Galveston (Tex.)—Social life and customs—Juvenile literature.
I. Title.
E185.93.T4N448 2010
394.263—dc22   2009005462

Manufactured in the United States of America
1 2 3 4 5 6 – DP – 15 14 13 12 11 10